# No More Running In Circles

## Study Guide

with notes
for group
leaders

by

Kim Engelmann

ISBN-13: 978-1493677139
ISBN-10: 1493677136

Printed in the United States of America

# Table of Contents

# Prologue

When you turn the page of this workbook and get started with the study guide, Kim Engelmann is going to give you both an outline and several compelling reasons for why you should take this book and gobble it up. But first, I want to tell you why you should trust her AND follow her advice.

In early 2008, someone sent me a copy of Kim's book, *Running In Circles*. I stayed up all night and read it (the first time) in one sitting. I used my limited ability to navigate the World Wide Web, found her email address (a miracle), and sent her an email. I don't normally behave like an internet stalker, but I simply had to tell Kim that her book touched my heart in ways that were too sacred to ignore. I thanked her for writing about her suffering while treating with respect those who had caused her harm; I expressed appreciation for the finesse and grace it must have taken to write about her suffering without sounding like she was a victim. She managed to convince me, the reader, that she told the truth without sugar-coating or shaming others. I figured she must be a woman of integrity. I never expected to hear from her, but she graciously wrote me back, and we've since found ways to connect. I consider it a grand privilege to call her my friend. I want you to know that you can trust the work she will ask you to do, because she herself has walked this same path. Kim is the real deal, and she is showing us how we can become "real" too. (Remember *The Velveteen Rabbit*? That kind of real…)

We can learn how to tell the truth, be our true in-Christ selves, and heal from the inevitable wounds that come from living on planet earth. Kim has included snippets of her book within the lessons you are about to start studying. But I encourage you to read the book as you work the lessons. It's just that good…

Blessings to you and yours as you take this study guide and apply its principles to your daily life!

Teresa McBean
Executive Director
National Association for Christian Recovery

# Introduction

## The Meaning of Christian Recovery

The word "recovery" is an active word—one that is happening in the present tense. It is also a word that implies an ongoing healing process that moves people from being in a state of sickness to a state of health.

If one uses the metaphor of the body, the wounds and offenses of the past are being "re-covered" (so to speak) as a scab is formed over a wound and gives way to new, fine skin. This coating or protection can succumb to wounding again at any time, especially during the early stage of healing. We can re-injure the area, and then the whole process starts over from the beginning. The human body naturally moves us toward wholeness and healing. Eventually, given enough time and proper attention, our physical wound is healed and covered with several layers of sturdy skin that can serve as a protective shield for our internal organs. Each time we wound ourselves, new recovery is an option, but the pain involved in incurring a new wound is inevitable.

## Progress, Not Perfection

Hopefully, this pain makes re-injuring ourselves undesirable. However, if we wound ourselves too often we can become numb to the pain or simply decide not to feel it. Once we are able to admit the pain, it acts as a guide for us. Pain is a gift; it is an invitation to consider recovering our lives.

Gradually, over time, we learn to stay away from things that cause the wounding. In terms of physical wounds, those things might be sharp objects or strenuous activity. Still, we never assume that we cannot be injured again. We might know what to avoid and how to keep ourselves safe, for the most part. However, ultimately, even from a physical perspective, we never reach a state where we become invulnerable to our environment. The human body is fragile. A bump on the head, a clog in the artery, and we can cease to exist. Although we would like to think that we are more resilient than we are, the truth is that our existence is a miracle that is dependent on the tender balance of our environment with our own internal biological state.

## Recovery and Spirituality

All of this runs parallel to our own recovery from addictions that mar and destroy our lives. The pain of addiction, when it causes continual wounding, can numb us to its effects. That is so often why some of us must hit bottom. It is a wake-up call to feel the pain and to recognize the devastation we are causing. It is a moment that teaches us to open our eyes, get real, and be honest. Climbing up from the bottom requires a dependence on God, who moves us toward healing and wholeness. This dependence is our deepest sense of spirituality. We recognize that our own recovery is fragile and tenuous. We never "arrive" at being immune to a relapse. Still, transformation happens, healing is possible, and as St. Paul writes, we "move from one state of glory to the next."

Recovery is active and present. We are always working on it, much the way someone who wants to get fit or be good at a sport is constantly "working out." Once we stop "working" our recovery, we will become flabby and easily succumb to relapse. But this does not mean that we need to be defined by our potential relapse. We are defined rather as children of God, who are first and foremost God's beloved. As God continues to help us, we recognize the miracle that life is, and the miracle of our own recovery. We learn to work our recovery one day at a time. The paradoxical nature of working our recovery and surrendering to God is the gist of this book. I need the spiritual disciplines and practices to help me grow into a fuller understanding of what it means to embrace life and live it well. As St. Ignatius put it, "Our only desire and our one choice should be this: I want and I choose what better leads to God's deepening his life in me."

As Christians (all Christians, including and perhaps especially those of us willing to admit our need for recovery), scriptures repeatedly point us to a life that is God-alert. To find the abundant life that Jesus alluded to in John 10:10 ("…*I have come that they may have life, and have it to the full.*"), the work of recovery provides us the opportunity to awaken to the possibility that a life of continual consciousness of the presence of God is the ultimate pathway to peace. Many of us have looked for our compulsions and addictions to provide that which only God can give.

> You keep in perfect peace
> whose mind is stayed on you,
> because he trusts in you.
> Isaiah 26:3

As we work together through this material, if we awaken and surrender to God's work in our lives, we begin to exhibit new behaviors that reflect this. Even though the substitutionary process will keep us clean and sober, from a theological perspective, the change can be even more profound. If we find ourselves growing in relationship to God and to his people in life-giving ways, we will begin to experience transformation—or as I have described it elsewhere, "second order change"—because of the work of the Holy Spirit alive in us. This goes beyond a change in behavior that "first order change" represents, which merely keeps us safe and on a straight and narrow path. Second order change is a new way to live abundantly and is what I call transformation.

## Recovery versus Sobriety

To illustrate, first order change is when we tweak the system within the same framework. If I am being chased by a monster, I do what I need to do to get away from the monster. I climb a tree. This can be analogous to the alcoholic who goes to AA instead of the bar—substituting one behavior for another. This is a beginning. Doing the next right thing. It is where we all must start, and where we must go when we are angry, lonely, or tired. Second order change is of a different ilk, and it is how I define transformation. Let's say that a monster is chasing me. I need to get away from that monster. However, instead of climbing a tree, I wake up from my nightmare. This "waking up" puts me in a new frame of reference. In my escape, I find myself on a whole new plane. Instead of tweaking within the system, I step outside the system and find my answer there.

## Awakening[1]

The waking up is, in a sense, the experience of the prodigal son who "comes to his senses" in the pigpen. It is also the experience of the addict or co-dependent who hits bottom and realizes, "I am powerless over this substance or behavior," and instead of trying harder within his/her context to survive, reaches outside himself to Someone beyond and surrenders.

Surrender is paradoxically the most powerful and most powerless stance for any of us, as we give up on human effort and reach out beyond our efforts to a Higher Power. For the Christian, it is Jesus Christ. Transformation also happens in countless ways as I continue to "wake up" to what God is doing in my life, "wake up" to the immensity of his grace time and again, and also begin to "wake up" more and more to the very sure and certain fact that my identity is not found in my disease but in my chosen-ness and beloved-ness as God's child.

## The Process

The question is always *how* then to best work our recovery so that we move toward transformation...not simply substituting a positive behavior for a negative one (although as I said this is a necessary practice and a good one) but experiencing a new perspective from a new frame of reference.

---

1. For further study, visit www.nacr.org for a series of videos on recovery and spirituality. These nine short (and long if you have the time for that version) videos might be helpful to show to your small group. In particular, I encourage you to watch "Waking Up" as it relates to this topic.

We will go back and forth between first order and second order change in our recovery. We will also "come to our senses" at many times on our recovery journey. We will continue to humbly recognize our failures and to glean new insights and perspectives. Substitution has its place to keep us on track, and it is effective in creating a healthy structure for ourselves. Still, living is all about relationships and developing trust, as well as experiencing joy.

If we are headed in the right direction toward healing and wholeness, deeper relationships with others, with God, and with ourselves will be the fruit. These relationships will gradually become far more fulfilling than our relationship with whatever addiction or co-dependent behavior we were facing before.

## What to expect

This study guide is designed to facilitate these kinds of life-giving relationships. My hope and prayer is that the transformation process will become the participant's reality, not just a concept. Facilitators and participants in recovery groups can use this study guide to assist in moving from first order change (where we simply substitute one behavior for another) to second order change (where fulfilling relationships with God, others and self puts us in a new place entirely).

1) I will use and continually refer back to the metaphors of the Hamster Wheel Lifestyle and Potter's Wheel Lifestyle to illustrate these two levels of change (Appendix A). The Potter's Wheel lifestyle is the one that leads us all into a continual process of transformation.

2) I also have used these metaphors in the companion book, *No More Running in Circles*. I highly recommend reading this book along with working through this study guide in a small group setting.

3) In addition to including these images as helpful metaphors, I offer spiritual exercises in each lesson to help the process of prayer and serenity take hold more fully. Allowing the Holy Spirit space to work and learning different ways to communicate with God is paramount as we seek the abundant life Jesus died to give us.

4) The section entitled "Going deeper in prayer" is a suggested daily practice in between sessions.

5) I have also included some notes especially for group leaders and facilitators. I hope these words encourage and support your ministry efforts.

May you be blessed as you engage fully in these lessons of liberation, hope, and entrée into Jesus' presence—that which transforms us all.

Kim

# LESSON 1

## Going Nowhere & Admitting It

*Step 1: We admitted we were powerless over our dependencies – that our lives had become unmanageable.*[2]

### Before we begin

Review the characteristics of Hamster Wheel versus Potter's Wheel chart (Appendix A).

Review the 12 steps (Appendix D) and any covenant bond your group has created around confidentiality, no cross-talk, etc. before each meeting. (A sample covenant is found in Appendix E.)

Icebreaker

Have you ever owned a hamster? What was the hamster's name? Did the hamster have a wheel? How much time did the hamster spend in the wheel?

How might the idea of a hamster running in a wheel be compared to the statement that is often coined in AA that insanity is "doing the same thing over and over and expecting a different result?"

### Introduction to the lesson

Only in the hamster world do hamsters know if they expect a different result each time they run in the wheel. However, people do expect different results even though they keep engaging in the same destructive patterns

---

2. Step one coincides with "going nowhere" - hamster wheel living (as opposed to the potter's wheel).

and addictions. The repeating of unhealthy patterns happens to us all, but it is a blind spot for many. It takes real effort to go a new way. Otherwise we go nowhere.

> If you were to give advice to someone on what to do to get off the hamster wheel and onto the potter's wheel, what would you say?

Each week we will refer to a metaphor that describes two different lifestyles. One is the hamster wheel lifestyle, and the other I call the potter's wheel way of life. We will continually use these two divergent ways of experiencing life for comparison's sake. Which way do you most identify with? Study these two frameworks for living as if your life depended upon it – because, frankly, it just may! (Turn to Appendix A and review the chart.)

Jesus often saw that people were going nowhere. They were going nowhere as they struggled with their illnesses, as they fought over religious practices, as they tried to seek revenge, or when they were upset about their lot in life. Jesus talked about a new paradigm, a different order, a new perspective. People did not always understand what he was talking about because he was coming from a heavenly perspective – not an earthly one.

> What new perspective do many people get when they "hit bottom?" Does surrender have a part to play? If so, in what way?

In your opinion, why might it be hard to surrender when you are on the hamster wheel?

What new perspectives and insights have you had as you have begun your journey of recovery? Is it different from what you experienced before you began this journey? Explain.

## Biblical Connect

Read Luke 15:11-31

Do you think the pigpen helps this son "come to his senses"? Why or why not?

Have you had any pigpens in your own life that have woken you up or brought you to a new awareness?

How was surrender a part of this process?

How is surrender different from simply giving up and doing nothing?

Being a piece of clay, surrendered to God's hand who molds and shapes us, is a common image in Scripture. Think of clay on a potter's wheel. It is not brittle. It is moist and pliable.

## Close with prayer

Spend a few moments in silence, and imagine a potter working on a piece of clay at a wheel. Imagine you are the clay and God is the Potter. Write down any thoughts or words that come to mind.

Turn to Appendices B and C to find the Lord's Prayer and the Serenity Prayer. Form a circle, hold hands, and pray both prayers in closing. Introduce the prayer by saying together, "Let the circle remind us that we do not have to do this work alone."

## Going deeper in prayer

Consider practicing this prayer several times this week...

Sit quietly for a few moments. Take some easy, deep breaths, allowing your heart and mind to become quiet. See yourself on a path. You are lost. You are uncertain. You long to know God as your true Father, but you anticipate disappointment and rejection. You look down the road and see someone running toward you. This One is moving fast. You realize to your shock that this One who runs toward you with joy is God. God's arms are stretched out toward you. God calls your name. You see joy on God's face. You hear God say "my child" to you. God is in front of you now, embracing you. Let God hold you. Take some time to tell God anything you want to say. Listen as God speaks love to you.[3]

---

3. Excerpted from *An Enduring Embrace*, by Juanita Ryan, Christian Recovery International, P.O. Box 215, Brea, CA 92822, pp.16-17.

# LESSON 2

## Disempowered or Empowered?

*Step 2: We came to believe that*

*a Power greater than ourselves*

*could restore us to sanity.*[4]

### Before we begin

Review the characteristics of Hamster Wheel versus Potter's Wheel chart (Appendix A).

Review the 12 steps (Appendix D) and any covenant bond your group has created around confidentiality, no cross-talk, etc. before each meeting. (A sample covenant is found in Appendix E.)

Icebreaker

Have you ever heard the statement said, usually in exasperation, "If I don't do it, it won't get done!"? Who do you remember that has said this to you or to someone you knew? Explain the context.

Do you think the person was right? Why or why not?

### Introduction to the lesson

Think about the hamster and the wheel. Does the hamster wheel move if the hamster is not inside the wheel making it move? The answer is "no." The wheel stands empty and static until the little hamster enters and with his small little legs, runs and runs. Then the wheel turns.

This hamster could say "If I don't do it, it won't get done. The wheel won't move round and round unless I make it happen."

---

4. Step two coincides with depletion on the hamster wheel versus empowered by God on the potter's wheel.

From our perspective we might answer back, "Yes, but you are going nowhere. It really does not matter if the hamster wheel goes around or not. You are getting depleted for something that doesn't really matter."

Do you think the hamster would believe us and stop his running in circles?

Are there things that you are doing right now, in your life, that are depleting?

Some may be necessary, but some may not be necessary. Or perhaps these things could be simplified in some way. Even if the things we are doing that are depleting seem necessary to us, they may not be necessary from God's perspective.

Share your thoughts on this with each other.

For each activity or thought pattern that you identify that is depleting, answer each of these questions…
    Is it necessary?

If so, what makes it necessary?

How might I simplify or make this task less depleting?

Does the clay on the Potter's Wheel make the wheel go around? Who does this, and how?

When in your own life have you experienced God's power "taking over" and providing you with power you did not have, to do the things you could not do, on your own?

How do you understand Step 2 – that a power greater than you can restore you to sanity? What does sanity mean for you?

## Biblical Connect

Read Mark 5:1-15

Before Jesus healed this man, the man was insane. Insanity is described in this story as being out of control. This is also the definition of someone who is addicted; out of control behavior is characteristic.

> "No one could restrain him anymore, even with a chain, for he had often been restrained with shackles and chains, but the chains he wrenched apart and the shackles he broke in pieces; and no one had any strength to subdue him."

After Jesus heals this man there is a sense of order and peace. The man is clothed and in his right mind. He is able to sit and be with Jesus. No one had any strength to subdue this man's insanity. He needed a power greater than his own to restore him to sanity.

Most of us are not running around breaking chains and bruising ourselves with rocks, but the power of addiction causes self-destructive behavior in many ways. When we do the same thing over and over while expecting a different result, we are on the hamster wheel. This kind of insanity produces frenetic out of control behavior. Jesus brings us peace and does a work in us that frees us from the hamster wheel.

Have you experienced peace (or partial peace) at this point in your journey of recovery?

On a scale of 1-10, 10 being orderly and 1 being chaotic, where would you rate a "typical" day of your life?

(Surrender doesn't necessarily mean peace right away or all the time. But peace and order will become more a part of our daily lives as we continue to depend on a power greater than ourselves to fashion and empower our lives.)

## Close with prayer

(Don't forget to form your circle and start each prayer with, "Let the circle remind us that we are not alone.")

Lord,
The world moves so fast
And I am fragile in it trying to keep pace
My desire for safety and security
Keeps me hard at work doing things that...
Should I pause and ponder my life
I might find unnecessary
Let me believe that it is okay to breathe deeply
And find an oasis of quiet in the center of myself
Where I can stop, consider, and pray
If I am on the wrong wheel, help me to get off
And surrender my busy-ness for your grace that
moves mountains. Amen.

## Going deeper in prayer

Consider practicing this prayer several times this week...

Here I am! I stand at the door and knock.
If anyone hears my voice and opens the door,
I will come in and eat with him and he with me.
Revelation 3:20

Sit quietly with this image of God knocking at the door of your life. Notice your responses to this image. When you are ready, respond to God's patient, respectful, loving initiative.[5]

---

5. Excerpted from *An Enduring Embrace*, Juanita Ryan, Christian Recovery International, P.O. Box 215, Brea, CA 92822, p. 13.

# LESSON 3

## Making Decisions

*Step 3: We made a decision to turn our will and our lives over to the care of God as we understood God.* [6]

### Before we begin

Review the characteristics of Hamster Wheel versus Potter's Wheel chart (Appendix A).

Review the 12 steps (Appendix D) and any covenant bond your group has created around confidentiality, no cross-talk, etc. before each meeting. (A sample covenant is found in Appendix E.)

Icebreaker

What was the best decision you ever made?

What was the worst one?

Did you ever make a decision that you thought was bad but turned out to be very good? Share together.

### Introduction to the lesson

God has always made a big deal about our human decisions and our free will. At first it might be hard to understand how a Power that is stronger than us would care about our little choices. The truth is, however, that our conscious choices are the difference between life or death for us. When we make the right choices, we align ourselves with God's power and love for us. When we make the wrong choices, we distance ourselves from God's

---

6. Step three coincides with the captivity of the hamster wheel versus having the awareness that we can choose another way.

power and love. The power is there. We hold the controls by the decisions we make.

When we decide to make a conscious choice to hand over our wills and our lives to God, that is the ultimate decision of a lifetime. Picture this. Imagine that God is at the center of life and creation, and we are all "rotating" around him. (Of course, later in our spiritual journey, we discover that God is not "stuck in the middle" of our understanding of him, but he is also at the circumference of our field of vision and beyond. But that's for another day!)

For today, we think of the decision like this: Step three is the decision to turn and face him. That's it. We just turn and face him. It doesn't mean we understand the implications or even necessarily have a changed "experience" with God. It doesn't mean we are full-on committed to believing that he exists or even what form his being takes. But we are deciding to stop running and turn towards God, even if in our turning the only thing we can understand at this moment is that we are surrendering all past assumptions about who God is and what he is (or is not) up to in our lives.

What is it about God that made it necessary for him to create us with the capacity to make decisions for or against him?

How does making a conscious decision allow us to recover a sense of who we are, for better or worse? (When we are under the influence of a substance, or in a codependent cycle, can we make a conscious decision that is truly our decision? Or are we making it from a distorted perspective that stems from our own captivity to addictive behavior?)

Sometimes the decisions we must make are hard ones! We must take stock of the true state of things and not let distorted thinking mask our problems. We must take life on life's terms. Otherwise we stay stuck in the hamster wheel.

If we can think about a situation in a way that helps us wrap our mind around it, it can definitely be helpful. But when our thinking becomes a way to distance ourselves from our feelings, we need to pause and take stock of our internal state.

"I've lost everything," someone recently confided in me. "My house, my family, my job - gone. But God wanted it this way, so that's it. All my days were planned ahead of time, the Scripture says. I've just got to realize that God's will must be done."

Honestly, this is all too slick and too quick for me to accept. It's like wallpapering a room when the plaster is crumbling underneath. Slap on a scripture! Slap on a happy face! Presto - the room is done. The building is falling apart, but it sure looks pretty. God conveniently gets blamed for a lot of things that are not his will at all.

Although my confidential informant sounds spiritually minded, I think this is really an example of rationalization. Rationalizing is a process where we come up with reasons that justify actions or consequences that are often the cause of our own poor choices. God is an easy target. If we can blame God rather than making clear distinctions and perhaps some difficult decisions, we can stay "stuck in the muck" of our own inertia—our hamster-wheel process.

How does making a conscious choice involve us in working our own recovery?

Is there a contradiction between working our recovery and surrendering our life and will to God? Explain.

The hamster runs in a circle because he is in a cage. There is no place else to go. He is hemmed in by a set of restraints that he cannot change. I remember once when someone left the door to our hamster cage open. Our hamster, Nugget, ran out in delight and began building a new home inside of our couch. He went back and forth from his cage to the couch, bringing food to store, with all the energy that he had used before to run in circles. In being set free, our hamster was able to go somewhere. (We let him live in the couch for awhile because he was just so happy and we tried not to sit on him!)

How is addiction a form of captivity?

There is an external captivity that might be the bars of a cage, or a certain set of expectations put on us by others that are destructive to us. There is also internal captivity. A phrase that is used in AA is, "Wherever you go, there you are."

What kind of captivity is this phrase referring to?

How does a conscious choice to turn over our will and lives to God set us free?

Why is the image of God holding us "with loving intent" on the potter's wheel important for us to remember as we give over our lives and will to the care of God?

## Biblical Connect

Read together Isaiah 29:16, Jeremiah 18:6, Isaiah 45:9, and Romans 9:21. (The language in these passages not only emphasizes God's sovereignty but also his ability to right a wrong, or purify a wayward nation, even if it means pain.)

Do you believe that the ultimate plan that God has for his children is good? (Try to avoid giving the "right" answer; share with your group your experience of God up to this point in your life.) Explain.

How do you make sense of the scriptural perspective and your personal experience?

Does this mean that we will be exempt from hardship and trial after we hand over our life and will to God? Explain.

A potter does not handle the clay he or she is holding lightly and gently. In order to get a lump of misshapen clay to be ready to be shaped into a vessel that is useful, the potter has to throw the clay down against the wheel again and again. This is to align the molecules in the clay so that when it is shaped it will not fall apart. Then, when the potter works with the clay to fashion it into a vessel, he/she applies tremendous pressure to the clay and holds it firmly in place so that it can be shaped correctly.

How does this description relate to the way God has worked in your life, if at all?

How does throwing the clay down and applying pressure to the clay, although seemingly harsh at first glance, demonstrate God's loving intent?

### Close with prayer
Form a circle, remind each other that, "The circle reminds us that we do not have to do this alone." Pray the Serenity Prayer (Appendix C).

### Going deeper in prayer
Consider practicing this prayer several times this week…

In a time of quiet, ask God to show you where you have closed your heart and mind to the possibility of prayer (and/or his work within you). Perhaps you feel that you do not know how to pray. Ask for the grace to be open in your weakness to allowing the Spirit to pray for you.[7]

---

7. Excerpted and adapted from An Enduring Embrace, by Juanita Ryan, Christian Recovery Internatiional, P.O. Box 215, Brea, CA 92822, p.20.

# LESSON 4

# Being Honest

*Step 4:  We made a searching and fearless
moral inventory of ourselves.*[8]

## Before we begin

Review the characteristics of Hamster Wheel versus Potter's Wheel chart (Appendix A).

Review the 12 steps (Appendix D) and any covenant bond your group has created around confidentiality, no cross-talk, etc. before each meeting. (A sample covenant is found in Appendix E.)

Icebreaker

Do you remember a time when you lied about something?

What was your reasoning for making the decision to lie?

---

8. Step four coincides with being honest about the fact that we need to get off the hamster wheel and onto the potter's wheel.

Were there consequences?

How did you cope?

## Introduction to the lesson

Humility that leads to honesty with ourselves is probably the greatest building block to spiritual growth. How hard it is to be brutally honest! How hard it is to take responsibility for our own actions and not to blame someone or something else! How hard it is to recognize that we need to get off the hamster wheel!

Doing an inventory is an exercise in honesty. (The Big Book has very specific guidelines on how to do an inventory, so we are not discussing this here. We also have study guides on the 4th step available through the NACR website – www.nacr.org.) In summary, an inventory is taking account of my own weaknesses and shortcomings and looking critically at how I am living my life.

Henri Nouwen wrote a great little book called *Can You Drink The Cup?* In it he talks about looking at our lives and essentially taking the time to ponder what we are living – in essence taking inventory. He writes the following:

"Holding the cup of life means looking critically at what we are living. This requires great courage because when we start looking, we might be terrified by what we see. Questions may arise that we don't know how to answer. Doubts may come up about things we thought we were sure about. Fear may emerge from unexpected places. We are tempted to say 'Let's just live life. All this thinking about it only makes things harder.' Still we intuitively know that without looking at life critically we lose our vision and our direction."

Familiar ways of doing things, even if they are unhealthy or destructive patterns, feel safe if we don't look too closely. [9]

What examples can you think of that might illustrate this concept?

How does looking critically at our lives (or taking an honest inventory) help us stay on track with who we want to be and with God's vision and direction for our lives? How do we find the courage to do this?

How might skipping Step 4 keep us on the Hamster Wheel? After all, the hamster wheel keeps us very busy!

Moving from the hamster's wheel to the potter's wheel can be frightening and disconcerting. We might be called to something unfamiliar and

---

9. This is s challenging concept; after all, how can we be conscious of our unconscious? If you go to www.nacr.org and avail yourself of the recovery and spirituality videos, it might help you sense a new and different way of "seeing".

challenging. Taking the time to look at our lives critically and doing an inventory that is honest and forthright will reveal things that often we'd rather not see. The temptation is to stay running in the hamster wheel so that we can easily avoid honest reflection. We just keep going and stay busy. This frenetic pace keeps us off the potter's wheel and safe from the pain of new formation. It also keeps us from being flexible in God's hand and recognizing the vision and direction God has for us. Inventory, holding our cup of life and looking at our lives critically, and being willing to change demands that we be honest.

What would it mean for you if you were completely honest when you came into the presence of God?

What might happen to your prayer life? Do you think your prayers might sound more like the book of Psalms that are brutally, one hundred percent, honest?

## Biblical Connect

Here are some statements from the book of Psalms. Have you ever used these statements in your prayer life?

Out of the depths I cry to you O Lord! (Psalm 130:1)

O that you would kill the wicked O God! (Psalm 139:19)

Search me, O God, and know my heart; test me and know my thoughts. (Psalm 140:23)

We might not think that it is theologically correct to ask God to kill the wicked. But the psalmist did not care if it was theologically correct or not. It was the place he was in, and he was all out honest before God with his feelings and concerns.

What are some statements that you make in prayer when you are being honest, open, and vulnerable before God? Write them below. Jesus honors the person who is honest and real. Our honesty and lack of pretense draws us onto the potter's wheel very quickly.

## Close with prayer

Join hands and make a circle. Begin the Lord's Prayer (Appendix B) with the following introduction, "Let the circle remind us that we do not have to do this work alone."

## Going deeper in prayer

Consider practicing this prayer several times this week...

> She gave this name to the Lord who spoke to her, you are the God who sees me, for she said, "I have now seen the One who sees me." Genesis 16:13

Sit quietly, breathing slowly, with your hands open on your lap in a receptive posture. Be aware of the Presence of kindness and compassion. Be aware that this is God with you, seeing you through eyes of love. Allow yourself to be seen by the One who sees you with compassion and delight.[10]

---

10. Excerpt from *An Enduring Embrace*, by Juanita Ryan, Christian Recovery International. P.O. Box 215, Brea, CA 92822, p.26.

# LESSON 5

## Someone With Skin On

*Step 5: We admitted to God, to ourselves and to another human being the exact nature of our wrongs.*[11]

### Before we begin

Review the characteristics of Hamster Wheel versus Potter's Wheel chart (Appendix A).

Review the 12 steps (Appendix D) and any covenant bond your group has created around confidentiality, no cross-talk, etc. before each meeting. (A sample covenant is found in Appendix E.)

Icebreaker

Did you ever think someone was really scary (maybe when you were a kid) and then after you had a conversation with them you realized that they were better than you thought? Share together.

When in scripture does Jesus ask people to "get real" and "fess up" to him or someone else? It actually happens quite frequently. See if, as a group, you can remember at least three incidences of this. (To get you started…think of the woman at the well in John 4:7-26. What did Jesus want her to admit?)

---

11. Coincides with step five by breaking the isolation of the hamster wheel and telling someone "with skin on" the truth!

## Introduction to the lesson

A child was scared at night. She could not sleep. Her mom told her that God was with her at which point the child replied, "Yes Mommy, I know. But I need someone with skin on."

It is sometimes easier to "fess up" to God than to a real human being with skin on. If we "fess up" to God we can keep the whole experience sort of abstract and "out there." Yet when we talk to a real human being and tell that person *everything* and that real human being forgives us and does not judge us, what a comfort and relief that is!

Have you ever had this experience? Share with the group.

One person, after admitting to her sponsor in AA the exact nature of her wrongs, was sure that the sponsor's reaction would be disapproval. Instead, after an intense sharing where the sponsor said nothing but just listened, the sponsor said to this individual "I loved you before, but I love you even more now." That is God's grace! What a relief it was to hear those words.

We all need to be forgiven and loved. When someone we know and trust embodies God's grace for us, it is so healing. Scripture tells us "Confess your sins *to one another* so that you may be healed." (James 5:16)

Do you have safe people in your life whom you can go to and confess (do an inventory)? Put their names below.

What are some qualities of safe people?

Why is it important to identify who the safe people are in our lives, before doing our inventory with them?

What pattern of the hamster wheel lifestyle are we breaking when we confess our sins, not just to God, but to one another?

What qualities in our character are required of us so that we can do this?

## Biblical Connect

Read John 8:10-11.

Think about Jesus saying those words directly to you. What is the look in his eyes?

What is the tone in his voice? Discuss together.

How do your brothers and sisters in the faith represent Jesus Christ to you?

What changes will you need to make in your life and daily practices in order for sharing your faults and shortcomings to become a continual practice?

In light of all that we are learning, why daily?

### Close with prayer

Form a circle, introduce the Lord's Prayer (Appendix B) by saying, "Let the circle remind us that we do not have to do this alone."

### Going deeper in prayer

Consider practicing this prayer several times this week...

Give ear to my words, O Lord, consider my sighing. Listen to my cry for help, my King and my God, for to you I pray. In the morning, O Lord, you hear my voice; in the morning I lay my requests before you and wait in expectation. Psalm 5:1-3

As you sit in quiet, reflect for a few moments on the-God-who-hears. Reflect on the-God-who-hears your sighs and cries for help with compassion. As you are ready, speak your heart to God. Thank God for hearing you today.

# LESSON 6

# Being Willing

*Step 6: We were entirely ready to have God remove all these defects of character.*[12]

## Before we begin

Review the characteristics of Hamster Wheel versus Potter's Wheel chart (Appendix A).

Review the 12 steps (Appendix D) and any covenant bond your group has created around confidentiality, no cross-talk, etc. before each meeting. (A sample covenant is found in Appendix E.)

Icebreaker

The Yield road sign means what?

How do you know when to break into traffic?

Have you ever been in a situation where it was hard to yield or you didn't want to yield? Explain.

---

12. Coincides with Step six; we allow God to transform us from the inside out.

## Introduction to the lesson

No matter where we are, no matter how badly we have messed up, no matter what our story, our pain, our grief—there is a Redeemer. There is always hope, because there is always Jesus. God is able to do "immeasurably more than all we ask or imagine." (Ephesians 3:20) God is able. However, we must be "entirely ready."

What does "entirely ready" mean for you as you think about your own desire for growth and change? Discuss together.

AA emphasizes that step six has a lot to do with our willingness to change—to admit our defects, to acknowledge our shortcomings, to own our own stuff—whatever it may be.

Interestingly, in scripture Jesus often asks people who are seeking his healing touch certain pertinent questions. He queries, "What do you want me to do for you?" In one case he asks this of a blind man who cries out in response, "Lord! I want to see!"

It seems that as we are transformed, healed, and made new, Jesus is very interested in having us articulate exactly what it is that we are willing to have him do for us.

Why do you think this is?

Do you think that putting our desires and longings into words and being as specific as possible is helpful when we pray? Why or why not?

There were often things that people needed to be willing to do in order to be changed and healed. One time Jesus told ten lepers to go and show themselves to the priests. Can you think of other things Jesus asked people to do in order to get healed or changed? Make a list.

When Jesus asked most of the people to do something (to help facilitate change or healing), they were for the most part READY AND WILLING.

But not always. One person who was not willing was the rich young ruler. He was very rich, and he was not willing to sell his belongings and give them to the poor. He went away sorrowful, in bondage to all that he had.

How does what Jesus asks us to do bring liberty?

How do our own ideas of what makes "the good life" or "what we should do" keep us in bondage? Or...

How does a hopeless attitude, a feeling of low self-worth paralyze us, or make us numb to what we really want? Or…

How might a feeling that God is aloof and not interested in our lives in a deeply personal way, cause us to keep from asking…or answering Jesus' question, "What do you want me to do for you?"

If God asked you today, "What do you want me to do for you?" what would you say? Write your answer in the blank below and be as specific as you can be. Share together if you want to.

Spend some time in silent prayer, lifting what you wrote on the lines above to the Lord. What might God be asking you to do in order to help this process begin to happen?

As you look at the response above, would you say that you are entirely ready to do what is necessary to allow God to work in your life? What might be some barriers or hesitations to fully following through on what God might be asking?

Remember the status of the clay on the Potter's Wheel? Is it hard and brittle, or moist and flexible? (The answer is obvious, right? But take some time to really think about this question – and why the answer, the real and true answer, could change your life.)

## Biblical Connect

Read Jeremiah 18 and 19.

When God asks Jeremiah to go down to the potter's house, Jeremiah observes that the pot being created is flawed. The potter "reworked it into another vessel, as seemed good to him" (Jeremiah 18:4).

The clay at this point is still malleable enough to be reshaped. In the next chapter, however, Jeremiah buys a pot that has already hardened (Jeremiah 19). It cannot be reformed. Jeremiah throws the pot down and it breaks into pieces, illustrating the impending destruction of Judah and Jerusalem. The hardened vessel cannot be used for God's purpose, so it is destroyed.

Prayer is what keeps us moist in God's hands - pliable, flexible, moldable, and usable. The rigid old patterns that would destroy us soften as we open ourselves to the presence of Jesus and make space for him in our lives, allowing him to take over.

Honest prayer, open prayer, heartfelt prayer is what keeps us flexible, moldable, pliable, and usable as well as postured to be transformed. Our dishonesty hardens us and in that hardened shape, we are useless.

Our flexibility = Our willingness

The degree to which we are willing is the degree to which God can transform us and remove our character defects.

## Close with prayer

Lord, keep me moldable and flexible in your hand
Willing to bend to your requests
Willing to acknowledge my own shortcomings
Allowing you to strengthen me as you work with
  me and remove my shortcomings and character
  defects
Allowing you to shape me into a vessel on your
  wheel
That can receive
That can be filled
That can hold in good things
That has a purpose
And that can take in what you are asking me to
  do,
and act upon it
Make me willing and supple, I pray, as I rest in
  your hand.
Amen.

Choose either the Lord's or Serenity Prayers, form your circle…pray!!


## Going deeper in prayer

Consider practicing this prayer several times this week…

Zechariah asked the angel, "How can I be sure of this?" Luke 1:18

Sometimes prayer is giving voice to our doubts. The things we long to believe may seem too much to hope for—too good to imagine. Even the thought that God might give us what we long for may leave us speechless. But when we (honestly) voice our doubts, we open a door for God's Spirit to respond with the gifts of grace, truth, and healing that we so desperately need. Prayer is talking with God about our doubts.

What are your deepest doubts? Voice these doubts to God. Invite God to respond to your doubts and uncertainties. Sit quietly, asking God's Spirit to reveal your longing for God. Let the feelings that accompany your longing come to the surface. As you are able, talk to God about your longing to know his presence.[13]

---

13. Excerpted from *An Enduring Embrace*, by Juanita Ryan, Christian Recovery International, P.O. Box 215, Brea, CA 92822, pp. 39, 40 and 43.

# LESSON 7

# Reaching Out For Help

*Step 7:  We humbly asked God to remove our shortcomings.*[14]

## Before we begin

Review the characteristics of Hamster Wheel versus Potter's Wheel chart (Appendix A).

Review the 12 steps (Appendix D) and any covenant bond your group has created around confidentiality, no cross-talk, etc. before each meeting. (A sample covenant is found in Appendix E.)

Icebreaker

Think of a time you asked for help or simply responded affirmatively when someone offered assistance in some way. For instance, maybe it was at the grocery store. A clerk asks you "Would you like help out?" and instead of saying "No I'm fine," you said "Yes, thank you." Share together times when you said "yes" to a helping hand or reached out for assistance.

Are you someone who usually asks for help?

---

14. Coincides with step seven, that we must allow God to transform us from the inside out.

Or…do you find that asking someone to help you with something, whether large or small, is generally something you don't do?

## Introduction to the lesson

When we "humbly" ask God to remove our shortcomings, we are asking for help. Asking for help means recognizing our own weakness. We have to be humble enough to ask for help. We have to be humble enough to know that we need help (that we actually have shortcomings that truly "miss the mark") and that we cannot get off the hamster wheel on our own. Sometimes this awareness comes when we "hit bottom." But a daily awareness of our shortcomings and need for God's help is essential for working our recovery every day.

## Biblical Connect

Read John 8:1-11

In this story the religious leaders are trying to trap Jesus and they are using a woman caught in adultery to do so. They are the "good" people – the religious people. Yet in some ways, the shame for them might be worse than the woman whose shortcomings are exposed for all to see.

Discuss this. Why do you suppose in some ways the shame of the religious leaders is greater than the woman caught in adultery? (Think about the child's story…The Emperor's New Clothes. What was the embarrassing realization?)

What is arrogant about what the religious leaders are doing? Do you think they are aware of their arrogance?

What is the requirement that Jesus puts before the religious leaders who want to stone the adulteress? How does this engender humility in them?

What is implied by the fact that Jesus stays, and one by one, beginning with the eldest, everyone else leaves? Who is left to pass judgment?

How does Jesus deal with this woman as the two are left standing there alone together?

How does this engender humility in the woman? Bring change?

## Close with prayer

Hold hands, remind each other the significance of this circle (we are not alone), pray both the Serenity and the Lord's Prayer (Appendices B and C).

## Going deeper in prayer

Consider practicing this prayer several times this week...

Close your eyes. Put yourself in either the place of the adulteress woman, or as a religious leader with a stone in your hand. If there is a situation in your life where you need to forgive someone, perhaps you might want to be the religious leader. If you are feeling shame or guilt, you may want to be the adulteress woman. See Jesus looking at you. For the religious leader, hear him say "He who is without sin among you, cast the first stone." For the adulteress, hear him say, "I do not condemn you. Go and sin no more." Rest in the awareness that Jesus' grace covers both the shortcomings we know we have, and those that we are entirely unaware of.

# LESSON 8

## Opening Our Eyes to See What Is

*Step 8: We made a list of all persons we had harmed and became willing to make amends to them all.*[15]

### Before we begin

Review the characteristics of Hamster Wheel versus Potter's Wheel chart (Appendix A).

Review the 12 steps (Appendix D) and any covenant bond your group has created around confidentiality, no cross-talk, etc. before each meeting. (A sample covenant is found in Appendix E.)

Icebreaker

Share a time when you were so scared that you covered your eyes because you didn't want to see what was going on.

### Introduction to the lesson

This lesson is about recognizing people we have hurt in the past and our need to reflect honestly on our past and take steps to make amends. If we are constantly going into the future doing, we don't have time to look at the wreckage we have left behind. We can't even fathom that our actions could have been hurtful because we are so caught up in our own world of surviving. After a while we are afraid to look at the past because of the amount of damage we may have done.

One of the most famous passages of scripture is John 3:16. (God so loved the world that he gave his only Son, so that everyone who believes in him won't perish but will have eternal life.) It is very familiar to Christians. In that same section however, Jesus mentions something else that is not so familiar. He says, "*As Moses lifted up the serpent in the wilderness, so the*

---

15. Coincides with step eight that we must make an effort to reach out to those we have harmed.

*Son of Man must be lifted up."* Jesus is referring to a time when the Hebrew people, wandering in the desert, were being bitten by snakes. Many were dying. God's command to Moses was to make a bronze serpent and put it on a pole. Whoever looked at the bronze serpent would be healed of their snake bite.

> Why do you think God asked the people to look at what they were most afraid of, so that they could be healed?

The very thing we fear the most, our own death and shortcomings, we are told to behold…look at what you fear! When we are not afraid to look at what we are most afraid of, and recognize its presence in our lives, healing comes.

Sometimes the hardest thing to do is to look at how we may have hurt other people and to come to terms with our own shortcomings. Still, we must look at all of it and be reminded that in being honest, and in coming to terms with what we have done, we are on the road to healing if we truly desire to change and make amends. This means getting off the hamster wheel.

I have used the hamster wheel metaphor for so long, and still new insights come from it. Recently someone mentioned to me that a hamster never reverses direction. It is always postured to go forward…never pausing or going back to reflect.

In order to make amends with those we have offended in the past, the humility of the last step (step 7) is essential to this one. We have to step off of the hamster wheel, pause, and take stock.

> Where have we been? And what is in the wake of where we have been? Is there is rubble we are afraid to look at? What is the benefit of looking at the rubble?

## Biblical Connect
Read Luke 19:1-10

Does Jesus ask Zacchaeus to make amends?

What does Jesus do that brings Zacchaeus to the point where he recognizes his own shortcomings and wants to do something about those he has hurt in the past?

Explain the phrase, "hurt people, hurt." Do you think that is true in Zacchaeus' case?

How does Zacchaeus resolve to make amends? Do you think Zacchaeus' plan reconciled him to others? How so?

Jesus' response to Zacchaeus' plan to make amends is that "salvation" had come to Zacchaeus' house. Explain.

What is it about Zacchaeus' resolve that brought salvation? What do you think salvation means?

The Zacchaeus story is told as IF he repented in ten easy verses. If the process were that quick and simple, I suppose more of us would be willing to actually do the work of making amends! My own experience has taught me that God is working with and in and through me, oftentimes for a long, long time before I become willing to take my next right step.

As preparation for this prayer exercise, first thank God for his willingness to work, whether we recognize his hand or not. Silently, together as a group, ask the Holy Spirit to remind you that you owe an amends. Then, pray the following:

> 1. Ask God to help you stop running forward, pause, and get off the hamster wheel so that you can reflect on the past.
>
> 2. Ask God to help you prayerfully look at the past without fear or guilt (knowing that you are forgiven and accepted by God) and bring to mind those people with whom you need to make amends, recognizing that this will bring healing. If you want to at this time, you may want to write down their names.
>
> 3. Pray for the strength to move forward and trust God with the risk of being honest and humble before others.
>
> 4. Look forward expectantly to the results of reconciliation and forgiveness.

Share any insights that you may have had.

## Close with prayer

Make your circle, remind each other why you form a circle, and pray both the Lord's and the Serenity Prayer (Appendix B and C).

## Going deeper in prayer

Consider practicing this prayer several times this week…

> When Jesus reached the spot,
> he looked up and said to him,
> "Zacchaeus, come down immediately.
> I must stay at your house today."
> So he came down at once and welcomed him gladly.
> Luke 19:5-6

Sit quietly and restfully. Breathe quietly. Imagine that Jesus is saying to you, "….come down immediately. I must stay at your house today." Think of all the efforts you are making to see a Power Greater than yourself in your daily life. Dare to dream that God is attentive to your cries for help. He is not far away. In fact, he has come to your home to receive your hospitality. Take a few minutes to realize that God believes you have something to offer him: welcome and joy and hospitality. Spend the rest of your time thanking God for this good news. You are a person whom God attends to. He trusts you to relate to him and to offer him respite and hospitality in loving relationship. You are a person of great worth in the eyes of God.

# LESSON 9

# Working at Loving

*Step 9: We made direct amends to such people wherever possible, except when to do so would injure them or others.*[16]

## Before we begin

Review the characteristics of Hamster Wheel versus Potter's Wheel chart (Appendix A).

Review the 12 steps (Appendix D) and any covenant bond your group has created around confidentiality, no cross-talk, etc. before each meeting. (A sample covenant is found in Appendix E.)

Icebreaker

Do you have a "to do" list in your head? What are some of the things that you want to get accomplished in the next few days? Are there any things that have been on that "to do" list for a bit too long?

## Introduction to the lesson

God declared in scripture (both Old and New Testament) that he loved people. In fact, his love for people was so great that he actually explained through the prophet Hosea that his love for Israel was like a man who falls in love with a woman only to find out that she has become a prostitute. Even then, God still takes her back and heals and mends the relationship.

---

16. Coincides with step nine where we are challenged to actually do something about what we know is wrong.

However, it isn't until God actually does something himself in sending Jesus, that people finally "get it." God acted in history himself, and now, when we look at the cross, we think of God's grace, forgiveness, and everlasting love. God did something personal in Jesus, and now we have a better understanding of his nature and character.

If Jesus (God in person) hadn't come, what do you imagine might be your perception of God? Would it be different or the same? (For some of us, we are still trying to figure out what we think about Jesus as God in person. If you're in that space, that's okay. A journey of faith isn't always about having the answer, as we said earlier – it's often about wrestling. Wrestling with this question is a fine, potter's wheel kind of response. God can handle our questions!)

When we make amends, why is it important that we do something…like actually going to the person and asking for forgiveness, in person, rather than just asking God to forgive us in our hearts?

Explain if you can the statement, "Love is something you do." Do you agree?

In the book of James, the emphasis is on "doing." "Do not merely listen to the word, and so deceive yourselves. Do what it says." (James 1:22). If that is so, how are we to live?

Have you ever thought about doing love in some way and then simply did not follow through? What prevented the follow through?

I have described the hamster wheel as a place where we keep going and doing and moving forward…going nowhere. How is the "doing" that James talks about different from the "doing" of the hamster wheel?

When have you followed through on "doing" love, either by making amends or in some other tangible way? Share together.

## Biblical Connect

Read John 13, John 18:15-18, 25-27 and John 21:15-19

In this story, we hear the story of Peter - a guy who is certain of his love for Jesus. In fact, he sounds a little defensive when confronted with the possibility of being the kind of person who could deny knowing the one he loves.

Jesus is proven correct in his assessment of the situation. Peter denies him not once, but three times, as Jesus predicted.   In the final scene of this recorded saga, Jesus seeks Peter out. He helps Peter make amends by appearing to him and conversing in a very intimate personal way.

It's difficult to know for sure what Peter was thinking during this exchange. It is possible that when Peter initially recognizes Jesus from the boat and springs into the sea, he does so because he wants to get there first and apologize. (We don't know, but it could well have been the case.)

Perhaps this is my own personal experience clouding my perspective, but as I read through this encounter, it does seem as if Peter struggles with the conversation.  Jesus helps Peter to make personal amends, face to face with him – but even with Jesus himself as the guide, amends making is difficult.

What do you think is important about a face-to-face encounter when making amends?

What are some of the steps Jesus takes Peter through in order for Peter to make amends? See if you can come up with your ideas about what actually happens in this encounter.

Jesus helps Peter to remember. Some people think that Jesus asked Peter three times, "Do you love me?" because Peter denied Christ three times. I am sure this was somewhat painful for Peter to remember that not just once, but three times, he denied Christ. Yet the memory is important so that the amends that we make can be done thoughtfully.

Jesus wants Peter's honesty. When Jesus asks Peter if he loves him, for the first two questions he uses the Greek word for love which is God's kind of love...all out sacrificial love. Jesus asks, "Peter, do you love me with all out sacrificial love?" Peter responds "Yes I love you" in response, but the word for love that Peter uses is far less grand. In Greek it means friendship kind of love. The third time Jesus asks Peter if he loves him, he uses the word Peter has been using to respond – the word for friendship love. Jesus asks the third time, "Peter, do you love me with friendship love?" Jesus meets Peter right where he is. He takes what he is willing to give. He has seen that Peter is now honest, and his assessment of what he can do is tempered by a realistic view of his own weaknesses. He is humble enough to acknowledge his own shortcomings.

Jesus promises a Potter's Wheel transformation. At the same time that Peter makes amends with Jesus humbly and honestly, Jesus promises him that one day he will actually *do* what he said he wanted to do (I will never deny you!), and instead of denying Christ....he will go to the death for him; Peter will follow through. In other words, one day Peter will love Christ with the kind of love that Jesus loves Peter with – all out "agape" or sacrificial love. Peter will not deny Jesus then but will stand up for him and will give his life. When we make amends, we acknowledge our own weakness to another. We admit that we have hurt them and ask for forgiveness. God's promise is that once we do this, honestly and openly, it opens the way for him to take our failures and fashion them on the Potter's Wheel so that we can become great lovers for his purposes.

## Close with prayer

Lord Jesus Christ have mercy on us
We are closed off to your presence so much of
the time
We gather in hope that you will let your
sacrificial love burn within us
We invite you to come to us...and as we follow
through to make amends
Open our eyes; we want to see you
Open our ears; we want to hear you
Open our hearts; we want to receive you
Open our minds; we want to know you
Open our hands; we want to serve you and DO
LOVE, following through with our words...
Lord Jesus Christ, have mercy on us
May your Potter's Wheel transformation happen
in us today.
Amen.

## Going deeper in prayer

Consider practicing this prayer several times this week...

Use the prayer above to begin a quiet time of sitting, listening,
breathing, and waiting upon the Lord. Allow yourself to sit and
receive from God. If your thoughts keep intruding, thank them for
coming, and gently return to attentiveness to your breath.

# LESSON 10

## Learning To Pray Our Inventory

*Step 10: We continued to take personal inventory and when we were wrong promptly admitted it.*[17]

### Before we begin

Review the characteristics of Hamster Wheel versus Potter's Wheel chart (Appendix A).

Review the 12 steps (Appendix D) and any covenant bond your group has created around confidentiality, no cross-talk, etc. before each meeting. (A sample covenant is found in Appendix E.)

Icebreaker

Did you ever have a plant that died because you stopped watering it? Or stopped giving it light? Share your stories. (If you have a green thumb, share with others how you do it!)

### Introduction to the lesson

We are never done with the process of growth. The Potter's Wheel whirrs continually throughout our lives, fashioning new designs and creating new things.

In order to cooperate with the movement of God's grace in our lives – staying moldable and flexible in God's hand - it is important that we continue to take stock of how we are living, making sure that we reflect on where we have been and where we are going. This exercise is important; it is like watering a plant, pulling up the weeds, and keeping the soil full of minerals. Doing inventory is like gardening…we've got to know what to do and what not to do to sustain growth.

We can take inventory on our own, or we can do it with God holding our hands. The ancient Christians figured out a long time ago how to take inventory through prayer. This lesson teaches you about this practice. It is called *The Prayer of Examen*.

---

17. Coincides with step ten where we are challenged to continually take inventory.

The Prayer of Examen allows us each night to go over our day and "examine" where we were "in step" with God's presence, and where we were "out of step." It allows us to see when we were "off" and when we were "on". It reveals to us our defects as well as our good moments. It's like doing a spiritual inventory and honest assessment every 24 hours. Below is an extended guide in order to do the Prayer of Examen.

## Biblical Connect

DIRECTIONS: Read through the description of the Prayer of Examen together as a group first. Discuss any questions that you may have. Then use the session to have each individual go and work through the Prayer of Examen privately. Have them reflect on their day.

Give the process of working through this prayer exercise about 30 minutes. When you come back together as a group, talk about your experiences, and covenant together as a group to do this prayer regularly for the next two weeks, individually before going to bed each night. In two weeks, take time to discuss how this is going and whether this exercise has been helpful.

## Prayer of Examen

The Prayer of Examen is a daily spiritual exercise developed by St. Ignatius of Loyola. This practice seeks to grow followers of Jesus in their capacity to discern God's will, find God in all things, and enhance their understanding of God's good creation. The prayer may take between 20 and 30 minutes. The majority of that time will be spent reviewing your day. Try not to dwell too long on thoughts. Instead, allow yourself to become aware and move on.
Begin by finding a quiet place where you won't be disturbed.

Then sit comfortably, with good posture and both feet on the floor. Allow yourself to relax and close your eyes if you like.

1. Recall you are in the presence of God. As you sit in silence, focus on God's deep and abiding love for you. We are always in the presence of God. Try to become aware of God's presence in an attentive way.

Ask the Holy Spirit to help you recall your day with love.

2. Then, recall your day with gratitude. After a few moments,

remember the small pleasures of your day: things like a good night's sleep, a good conversation, or a beautiful sunset. These are all gifts from God, and this practice fosters an "attitude of gratitude."

As you remember these small gifts from God, take a moment to reflect on the gifts that you gave today, whether to God or to others. How did you bring your strengths, your sense of humor, your abilities, your encouragement, or your patience to others today? When you have finished, pause briefly and thank God for these things.

3. Ask for guidance from the Holy Spirit. In a moment you will begin to retrace the steps of your day. Before you do, ask the Holy Spirit to guide and direct your mind. The Spirit will lead and guide you into the truth and mystery of your heart. Ask the Holy Spirit for the capacity to recall your day with clarity and an understanding of your limitations.

4. Review your day. This is the central and longest step of the prayer. Go back to the start of your day and allow it to play like a short movie in your mind. Pay attention to the details. What were your feelings? What motivated you to respond to certain situations in the way that you did? The purpose of this is to draw out the positive and the negative aspects of your day.

As you are reviewing your day, ask the question, "Where did I fail today?" Was there a moment when you lived out of anger or bitterness? Were there things that you avoided? Don't allow yourself to dwell on these things or seek to resolve them. Simply allow yourself to identify them and move on.

Next, ask the question, "When did I love?" Was there a moment, or several moments, in which you made the choice to live out of love? Perhaps it was a kind act like holding the door or spending intentional time with your family. Remember the ways that you chose to love this day.

Next, search for any patterns or habits during the course of the day. Do you make coffee at the same time? Do you chat for a few minutes with a coworker? Are you always staying late at work? As you detect these patterns, what emotions do you sense coming to the surface for each habit? Do these habits help you face your day with love? Do they hinder you from facing your day with love?

4. Reconcile and Resolve:

Finally, picture yourself seated next to Jesus, talking as you would with a friend. Maybe there was something in your day that you don't feel good about. Tell Jesus about this and express your disappointment and ask him to be with you when you face that moment again. Allow yourself to feel the sorrow in your heart as you share this, but also remember and give thanks for Christ's continual restoration of your heart. Remember all of the good moments of your day and thank Jesus for His presence with you in those moments.

6. End with the Lord's Prayer

"Our Father, who art in heaven, hallowed be your name. Your kingdom come, your will be done on earth as it is in heaven. Give us today our daily bread. Forgive us our debts, as we have forgiven our debtors. And lead us not into temptation, but deliver us from evil." Amen.

After 30 minutes, gather together to discuss your experiences with doing the Prayer of Examen.

## Close with prayer

Gather in your circle, remind each other that you are not alone, and pray the Serenity Prayer (Appendix C) together.

## Going deeper in prayer

Consider using the Examen at the close of your day several times this week.

# LESSON 11

# Learning to Connect With God

*Step 11: We sought through prayer and meditation
to improve our conscious contact with God
as we understood God, praying only for knowledge of
God's will for us and the power to carry that out.*[18]

## Before we begin

Review the characteristics of Hamster Wheel versus Potter's Wheel chart (Appendix A).

Review the 12 steps (Appendix D) and any covenant bond your group has created around confidentiality, no cross-talk, etc. before each meeting. (A sample covenant is found in Appendix E.)

Icebreaker

Share together some of the challenges involved in developing a rich prayer life. Perhaps it may be time issues. Or it may be that your mind wanders, and it is hard to focus when you pray.

What do you think about when your mind wanders and you are "supposed" to be praying? Think of the funniest thought you've had.

---

18. Coincides with step eleven where we are asked to improve our conscious contact with God.

## Introduction to the lesson

Most of us want to develop a rich prayer life. God is calling us to be in communion with him. His call always comes first. Our response is one of prayer – answering the phone that is ringing. However, sometimes when my teenager gives me his cell phone, and it is ringing, I don't know how to answer it. It looks too complicated for me to figure out. When he explains that all I have to do is slide over a little bar on the screen, it suddenly becomes manageable and even simple. Over time, I don't even think about how to do it.

A lot of times, prayer seems like a big mystery. We may have been Christians for quite a while, but prayer seems to elude us. We do it because we know we should, but it is not something we look forward to or get much out of. This lesson is about learning some creative ways to pray. Once you learn some of these exercises, prayer may actually become an enjoyable love relationship with the Almighty. It is all very simple, and requires only a willingness to try.

For this lesson you will stay together as a group and experiment with these different forms of prayer together. Communal prayer is something we have lost from our Jewish heritage. For the Jews, communal prayer was even more sacred than individual prayer, because in the larger group everyone's prayers balanced out everyone else's. There was no room to get lost in one's subjectivity. If someone was praying for individual concerns, someone else would remember to pray for the world, etc. Actually, many of these exercises can be used both with groups or individually. Doing prayer in a group, if it is done well, can actually help with focus, and the experience can be rich. Spend about 20 minutes on each prayer exercise given. Then share together your thoughts—what was meaningful, challenging, or difficult.

## Biblical Connect

(Leaders:  please read the leader's notes before group!)
The scripture for this lesson is from Philippians 4:6-7:

> "Do not be anxious about anything, but in every situation, by prayer and petition with thanksgiving, present your requests to God. And the peace of God (the serenity), which transcends all understanding, will guard your hearts and your minds in Christ Jesus."

## OPENING PRAYER EXERCISE 1:  (10-20 min.) God's Light

Give everyone a votive candle (or any free standing candle) as they arrive. Have each person light their own candle and spend some quiet moments watching the candles burn. Let the flame represent God's holiness and God's light that exposes all things. Praise God for a while (either aloud or silently) that he is the light, that he purifies and brings illumination, and that his light never gets extinguished. Praise him that because of Jesus, humanity does not have to walk in darkness any longer.

Observe that as the candle burns, it gets deeper at the core. With the candles still lit, pray together either in silence or out loud as a group for God to burn away anything inauthentic or superficial that may be distancing you from him or from others. Confess any sins you may be aware of in this area silently. Then invite Jesus to come into your gathering and illuminate to you ways that you can grow in authenticity and depth as a community. Ask that God burn away anything that is getting in the way of all of you together experiencing the fullness of his love. Allow the candles to burn throughout the group time together and have people take their candles home as a reminder of God's longing to burn away superficiality and sin—making us deep and authentic in our relationships with one another.

Discuss together this experience of prayer.

# GROUP PRAYER EXERCISE 2:  (10-20 min.) Praying Scripture

Start out with a unison scripture that can be read together. Psalms are a great choice. For this particular lesson, as you get started, try using Psalm 139 or Psalm 23. These are Psalms that are often familiar or at least easy to understand. To avoid the rote mindless recitation of empty words, which happens sometimes when we read the scriptures, everyone should read the psalm through silently on their own first. Then read it aloud slowly, together as a group, pausing wherever appropriate. Try not to have too much commentary on what the verses mean. Simply absorb the scripture as you would a worship song. As you read the psalm together in a prayerful manner, recognize that these are God's words to you. He has made the first contact and is speaking through the words on the printed page (or phone) to your heart. In doing this exercise, you are improving your conscious contact with God in spades. Sometimes soft music in the background helps to create a holy mood of centered calmness, receptivity, and an awareness of God's nearness as you read scripture aloud together. Close this segment of "praying the scripture" by passing the peace to each other, looking into the other person's eyes and shaking his or her hand. Remember that when you look into the eyes of your sister or brother, you also are looking into the eyes of Christ himself.

Discuss together this experience of prayer.

## GROUP PRAYER EXERCISE 3: (10-20 min.)   Heartbeat Prayer

Grow quiet together as a group and have each person become aware of his or her own heartbeat. Sometimes it helps to feel your pulse, either in your wrist or on the side of your neck. The heart is the center of our being, an organ that keeps pumping even when we are not thinking about it. This all-important, life-giving source can remind us of our Creator. Spiritual life gets pumped through us as we allow God to be at the center of our day. Like the heart that constantly pumps, God is loving us constantly, even when we are not thinking about him.

Praise God for the fact that he has given you life and continues to sustain you even when you are not thinking about it. Close your eyes now, and imagine that your heart is a prayer room, where Jesus can enter. You can think about Jesus entering your heart in many ways. It may be that you think about this as a light flooding your chest; maybe it is easier for you to think about the words of Jesus, "Abide in me," being literally pumped out from the center of your being. Whatever image helps you to "center" on Jesus, to rest in him as the Source of your life – focus on that. Ask Jesus to take away any sin that is separating you from him. Ask him to forgive you and clean up your heart, which is ultimately his home. Then see this expanding out to others in the group. See them awash in God's love and light. Simply whisper "Come Lord Jesus…Come into our fellowship… We invite you…Stay with us…For the hour is late, and we need your companionship."

Discuss together this experience of prayer.

# GROUP PRAYER EXERCISE 4: Using Symbols

Set in the center of the group a symbol as a focal point. When people's minds start to wander (which everyone says theirs does), it is a place to look that helps with focus. It might be a cross, a goblet with a loaf of bread, or even an open Bible. As you posture yourself to be attentive to God, you can look at the symbol and recognize it as a reminder of God's presence in the center of your group. You can tell people that because you are using a symbol, you all are going to pray with eyes open...not closed!

One great way to introduce symbols as a focal point for prayer is to use a stone representing Christ as the "cornerstone." Find a large rock that is fairly smooth and pass it around so everyone can write his or her name on it. When all the names of the group members are written on the stone, put it in the middle of the table as the focal point. Recognize together that all of you are joined as brothers and sisters by the strong and certain rock solid truth of Christ's eternal presence with us now.

As the group looks at the rock with all of the names written on it, offer up prayers for one another.

Discuss together this experience of prayer.

## GROUP PRAYER EXERCISE 5:  Guided Meditation

Download one of the guided meditations on biblical texts at:

http://www.nacr.org/nacr-store/audio-seminars

During your group time read the relevant scripture and then follow the imagery associated with the scripture. Before you play the meditation, encourage people to get comfortable, relax, and open their palms in their laps as a bodily gesture of receptivity.

Discuss together this prayer experience.

## GROUP PRAYER EXERCISE 6: A Stone Before a Sculptor

Brother Lawrence describes his prayer life in the following way:

> "Sometimes I imagine myself as a stone before a sculptor from which he will carve a beautiful statue. Presenting myself before God, I ask him to form his perfect image in my soul and make me entirely like himself."

Lead your group to come into God's presence by having people imagine themselves as a stone. If you want, you can even hand people some sharp or misshapen rocks to hold when they come in. As people hold the stones, have them silently or aloud ask God to carve something beautiful and meaningful out of the rock—to smooth down any sharp edges and take the shapelessness and create from it an image of meaning and purpose.

What would you like God to carve away? Let the group respond to this question in prayer, either silently or aloud.

What would you like God to carve into you? Let the group respond to this question in prayer, either silently or aloud.

Stay for a moment in the Lord's presence, waiting….allow about one minute of silence.

Praise God that he is the Master Sculptor and able to shape even stones into masterpieces for his use. Let the group bring their praises to God for this.

Read 1 Peter 2:5 as a great scripture on community, joint purpose, and calling. "You also like living stones, are being built into a spiritual house to be a holy priesthood…"

Variations on this exercise can involve handing group members clay or play dough as they arrive, and asking them to knead it in their hands as they pray and invite Jesus into their gathering. The prayer here would be to have God fashion the group in such a way that all participants together would be conduits for the presence of God and represent the body of Christ.

A fun thing to do afterward is to put everyone's piece of clay together to form a joint sculpture of the group that symbolizes unity and being open and receptive to God's presence. This sculpture, fashioned together, can be a focal point for the group. It doesn't have to be perfect—just symbolic and representative of everyone's participation together and willingness to be open to what God wants to do in and through them. Sometimes the sculpture comes out looking ridiculous, but it helps everyone not take themselves too seriously. It reminds the group that God uses us in our weakness…we are all "cracked pots" and all of us are a work in progress.

Discuss together this prayer exercise.

### Close with prayer
Circle up and pray the Serenity Prayer in unison.

### Going deeper in prayer
Consider practicing this prayer several times this week.

# Lesson 12

# Sharing the New Reality

*Step 12: Having had a spiritual awakening*
*as the result of these steps,*
*we tried to carry this message to other addicts,*
*and to practice these principles in all our affairs.*[19]

## Before we begin

Review the characteristics of Hamster Wheel versus Potter's Wheel chart (Appendix A).

Review the 12 steps (Appendix D) and any covenant bond your group has created around confidentiality, no cross-talk, etc. before each meeting. (A sample covenant is found in Appendix E.)

Icebreaker

What was the most exciting thing that happened to you in the last month that you couldn't keep quiet about? You just had to share it with someone else!

## Introduction to the Lesson

Everyone talks about his or her favorite restaurant, the best bargain store, the quickest shortcut that avoids traffic, the latest and greatest technological conveniences acquired, etc. This is all good news. We want to share it and to have others participate in it.

Why not the same for our recovery and transformation? Why not share it eagerly, especially with the epidemic of addictions that are so pervasive and definitive of our current culture? So many are bound by it, and so many are suffering.

We have resources to share. We know that there is hope, even in the most hopeless situations. We know a different reality from the reality of

---

19. Coincides with Step 12 where we are told to spread the good news of recovery and healing that we are living.

addiction and co-dependence.

Stephanie Brown is an author, researcher and a clinical psychologist in the area of addiction. She runs the Addictions Institute in Menlo Park, CA, and is herself a recovering alcoholic. She says the following:

> "I entered a different reality when I recognized my own alcoholism. Then, my entire world and my reality, the way I looked at myself and others, changed. Everything I've written about for all these years has a very central focus on reality and what is reality. In the actively addicted person and family, there is such a distortion about what's real."

As we have journeyed through the 12 Steps together in this workbook, we have come to terms with a new reality. The beauty of the 12 steps is that they cut away at all pretenses and help us to recognize the distortions that for years defined our reality. When you admit you are addicted, or co-dependent, or that you need help with any addiction, you come against the distortions that formerly skewed our perspectives and made us crazy. When the 12 steps are worked with integrity, you become honest and humble very quickly.

When we couple the 12 steps with a Christian perspective, it gives us tremendous hope. As we apply the scripture to the 12 steps, we learn that there is actually great help and complete healing available from Jesus Christ. We are more than alcoholics, co-dependents, and people lost in a web of addiction. We are primarily beloved children of God with a future and hope as bright as His promises. This is good news!

When your eyes are opened to this new reality, everything looks different, and joy replaces despair.

> If you could sum up the message of hope that Christ gives us to another person caught in addictive or co-dependent behavior, how would you share this new reality? What words would you say? What actions would you employ?

## ROLE PLAY

Have group members role play. One person shares his or her journey of hope (this new reality) with someone else who acts the part of a listless addict or hopeless wounded person.

What is the best way to share with others the good news of recovery and transformation?

What are the challenges?

What are the blessings?

Think about whom you are sharing the good news with today. Do you need to follow up?

Are there more people who might need to hear your story?

## Biblical Connect

Read Acts 9:10-22.

What was Ananias concerned about when God asked him to open Saul's eyes?

How did the Lord encourage Ananias to proceed?

Do you think the opening of Saul's physical eyes was a symbol of a greater transformation? Explain.

What does Saul immediately begin to do? (What does the first part of verse 20 say?)

How might this be instructive to those of us who are still at the beginning of our journey to know Christ more deeply?

What is one way that you can tell your story of God's goodness this week with someone who needs to hear it? Share together.

If you are able, after the discussion, sing together as a group the first stanza of Amazing Grace.

     Amazing Grace! How sweet the sound!
     That saved a wretch like me.
     I once was lost, but now am found
     Was blind, but now I see!

## Close with prayer

*(If there were certain prayer exercises in the last lesson that were especially helpful, you may want to incorporate this into the lesson as well, asking God to give everyone courage to share the good news with those in need.)*

As usual, circle up and pray the Lord's prayer.

## Appendix A

## Two Lifestyles

| Hamster Wheel Lifestyle | Potter Wheel Lifestyle |
|---|---|
| We experience life in isolation. | We are aware that God's hand is involved in the process of formation. He is in charge and we are never alone. |
| Our daily life is depleting and marked by unproductive suffering. | God's work is dynamic; it is transformational. We get off the wheel in a different shape and in a different place than when we got on. We are hopeful. |
| It seems like our lives are going nowhere (even though it feels like a lot is happening and can be chaotic, or very controlled to the point of rigidity). | We acknowledge that surrender, not willpower, is the key. As clay is kept soft during the molding process, our surrender to God keeps us flexible in his hand. We are humbly open to change. |
| Our life is experienced within a limited perspective; our frame of reference has neither new insights nor do we have energy to consider other options. | Often we may experience an awareness that we are being held with loving intent. We may even get a glimpse of God's larger perspective when we are on this wheel. |
| Our life feels like we are in prison. We have no hope for change. We lack creative energy and enthusiasm for change. | The outcome brings new life for us and for those around us. We have gone somewhere and become something new. Even if circumstances have remained unchanged, we have been liberated. |
| It is often done at night (anyone with a pet hamster knows this!) | We find ourselves on the Potter's wheel not only with God's hand in the mix, but also within the context of meaningful community. |

## Appendix B

Our Father who is in heaven,
uphold the holiness of your name.
 Bring in your kingdom
so that your will is done on earth as it's done in heaven.
Give us the bread we need for today.
 Forgive us for the ways we have wronged you,
just as we also forgive those who have wronged us.
 And don't lead us into temptation,
but rescue us from the evil one.
Matthew 6:9(b) – 13
Common English Bible Translation



Our Father in heaven,
hallowed be your name,
your kingdom come,
your will be done,
 on earth as it is in heaven.
Give us today our daily bread.
And forgive us our debts,
 as we also have forgiven our debtors.
And lead us not into temptation,
but deliver us from the evil one.
Matthew 6:9(b) – 13
New International Version

## Appendix C

The Serenity Prayer
God, give us grace to accept with serenity
the things that cannot be changed,
Courage to change the things
which should be changed,
and the wisdom to distinguish
the one from the other.
Living one day at a time,
Enjoying one moment at a time,
Accepting hardship as a pathway to peace,
Taking, as Jesus did,
This sinful world as it is,
Not as I would have it,
Trusting that You will make all things right,
If I surrender to Your will,
So that I may be reasonably happy in this life,
And supremely happy with You forever in the next.
Amen.

# Appendix D
## The Twelve Steps

Step 1: We admitted that we were powerless over our dependencies and that our life had become unmanageable.

Step 2: We came to believe that a power greater than ourselves could restore us to sanity.

Step 3: We made a decision to turn our life and will over to the care of God as we understand him.

Step 4: We made a searching and fearless moral inventory of ourselves.

Step 5: We admitted to God, to ourselves, and to another human being the exact nature of our wrongs.

Step 6: We were entirely ready to have God remove all these defects of character.

Step 7: We humbly asked him to remove our shortcomings.

Step 8: We made a list of all persons we had harmed and became willing to make amends to them all.

Step 9: We made direct amends to such people wherever possible, except when to do so would injure them or others.

Step 10: We continued to take personal inventory, and when we were wrong, promptly admitted it.

Step 11: We sought through prayer and meditation to improve our conscious contact with God, praying only for knowledge of his will for us and the power to carry it out.

Step 12: Having had a spiritual awakening, we tried to carry this message to others and to practice these principles in all our affairs.

This version of the Twelve Steps differs from the version used by Alcoholics Anonymous only in replacement of the word "alcohol" in Step 1 with the phrase "our dependencies". The Twelve Steps are reprinted with permission of Alcoholics Anonymous World Services, Inc. Permission to reprint and adapt the Twelve Steps does not mean that A.A. has reviewed or approved the contents of this publication, nor that A.A. agrees with the views expressed herein. A.A. is a program of recovery from alcoholism only: use of the Twelve Steps in connection with programs and activities that are patterned after A.A., but that address other problems, does not imply otherwise.

# Appendix E

## Sample Group Covenant

Any effective support group has guidelines for safety. Read these each week before each session as a reminder to the group of the appropriate boundaries attenders follow.

1. What is said in the room stays in the room; confidentiality is a covenant promise. (The only exception is if someone in the group indicates that they may be a danger to themselves or others. If this occurs, the facilitator will seek outside professional guidance for follow up.)

2. We do not offer advice or "cross talk" – meaning, when a participant shares, the rest of the group listens and expresses gratitude for the sharing. No one turns to the participant and offers suggestions/advice/criticisms or critiques.

3. We respect the group process by being mindful of the time and the number of participants.

4. Silence is golden and provides introverts an opportunity to process before speaking. It is okay to sit in silence.

5. We do not interrupt or talk "over" each other.

6. We listen when someone is sharing, and we respect their words and pay attention without distracting them or the group (turn off cell phones, don't talk with one's neighbor, etc.).

# Leader/Facilitator Notes

Before beginning the group: Familiarize yourself with the materials. This is an in-depth study, but it has been created for flexibility. Here are the components; as a leader you will make the call as to how many of them to utilize.

1. *No More Running In Circles* is a companion book that group attenders can read. I pray that in sharing my story, it will help others relate and perhaps gain new insights into their own stories as a result of reading about my healing journey.

2. Each group will need to make a decision about their covenant bond. A sample is provided, but I recommend that you have members sign and review before each meeting whatever covenant the group creates.

3. The *Biblical Connect* and *Going Deeper in Prayer* sections can be used by participants as study guides and daily reminders of the material they covered in the previous week's group meeting.

4. Facilitators can help structure the group's plan for using these various materials. Consider making the first meeting session a time for making these decisions as well as introducing participants to each other. As groups "own" the process they want to commit to, it will help set expectations and allow for the group to choose a pace that best suits the needs of the attenders.[20]

## Session 1

Structure and repetition are important for any recovery ministry. There is safety for the participant to know beyond a shadow of a doubt that a group is meeting no matter what, that the format will stay the same and that certain parameters (like the 12 steps) will guide the process. Sometimes, those of us who lead these kinds of ministries can become burned out by the seemingly endless repetition of the same message.

---

20. One format that others have appreciated goes like this: thirty minutes before the study session for anyone who wants to warm up with conversation with others, an hour of the group study, and a concluding thirty minutes of wrap up conversation. This allows for personal time to talk, and helps the group stay "on point" during the hour study. It also allows for those who cannot be there the entire two hours have some time flexibility with the optional thirty minutes before and after the study.

Repetition, structure and safety make up the scaffolding of the recovery process (and the transformation process as well). There are 12 steps, there are meetings, and there are certain things we must do as Christians. But it is not all the same. As we restate these same truths at the beginning of each meeting, new insights emerge. This is much like reading the same scripture you memorized years ago and gaining new insight. It is much like the two disciples on the Emmaus Road suddenly recognizing Jesus when he had been with them all along. Nothing had changed. They just saw things differently and had an "aha" moment.

In leading recovery ministries, facilitating support groups, and even when pastoring a church, it is important to find the "new" life in what becomes a pretty demanding routine, to celebrate small victories, and to see each story that is shared as a unique venue through which God can show up (or already has shown up). Each person's story is a journey that God longs to be a part of. Moving people toward the potter's wheel lifestyle means making that journey a sacred journey, not just for the participant, but for you as facilitator/leader as well. That is why celebrating the small victories is so crucial. It keeps us flexible, joyful, and surrendered to God's timing. Anything real and worth its salt takes time! So be encouraged and know that there is new life embedded in the routine.

## Session 2

The structure and order that you provide (talked about last time) in the recovery ministry is ushering in sanity to lives that are out of control. That is why order and repetition are so important. The order and structure you provide is a haven in the midst of a hamster-wheel existence. However, as leaders we too must surrender. It is not up to us to change people or keep them sober. As we all know, this is a decision and commitment that each individual must make for themselves. We can support and guide and pray. We are not in this area of ministry to act out our co-dependence or enabling tactics. We are in this ministry to set up a constructive framework so that God can do his best. Only God, because he is more powerful than we are, can change a life. Only God has the ability to bring us sanity. Although we love the people we work for and with, we must constantly give them back to God, trusting that he holds them and loves them more than we do. This surrender of not just our own lives, but the lives of those we work with and love is one of the hardest things we must learn to do as leaders. As we let go of the outcome and allow ourselves the liberty of a detached yet caring presence, we often find that the Holy Spirit is able to have some space to work in ways far more profound than what we could ever imagine.

O Lord,
Allow us to trust in you as we lead
Smooth our furrowed brow
Soothe our deepest worries with the balm of your mercy
Find us in the midst of our responsibilities and concerns
And assure us that you are actually in charge
For us
For others whom we love
For your world that you love
May we know the truth that has been sung for generations
That....Great is your faithfulness – is a truth that we can stake our
lives on. Amen.

## Session 3

A big hurdle and potential for misunderstanding, particularly with a
Christian Recovery Group, is the whole concept that we are surrendering
our lives to God "as we understand him." This statement allows all people
to engage with a higher power regardless of their persuasions. This is
genius!

One reality that all groups, individuals, and ministry leaders wrestle
with is that our understandings of God may be wrongheaded, confused,
or distorted. We may even have lots of good theological training and
know sound doctrinal truths, but underneath all that knowing we may
experience God as a severe taskmaster, a punitive judge, an unyielding or
absent parent, or an authoritarian dictator.

I might not say it out loud or even realize I believe it, but deep down,
if authorities in my past have not been benevolent to me, my image of
God is distorted. I can have trouble trusting in God's steadfast love. Even
"Christian" believers hang on to these idolatrous images that have been
fostered in childhood.

Returning to the introductory comments: this would be considered first-
order change. I am simply substituting my understanding of God for a
parent or other person of authority. When I am transformed...or when I
experience grace or second-order change, I grasp hold of the "out of this
world" love of God that surpasses any knowledge that I could ever have of
what genuine love could be like.

God's goodness is beyond what this life calls "good". God is **very, very**
good and blows my mind with his goodness. God loves me deeply and

steadfastly, and God does not judge me or gauge his love for me based upon my behavior. GOD IS LOVE all the time, and just for me, even if I was the only one alive. I must experience grace to take hold of this truth, but it is the crux of transformation.

As facilitators, wisdom prevails when we attend to this reality, showing exceptional sensitivity and alertness to the various assumptions (many unconscious) that are arriving in the room with each individual. Our job is not to fix. Our work involves empathetic guiding of the group.

Additionally, we need to have our own accountability structure that helps us process our own unconscious and off-base beliefs about God, others, and ourselves. (These may become apparent as we notice how we are unable to stay fully present, attending to the group's needs rather than our own. Group work has a way of bringing to light the areas where the leader needs work. This is both a good and God thing. It is only dangerous if we aren't able to acknowledge it and deal with it appropriately.)

## Session 4

As many of you already know, steps four and five are often where people get stuck in 12-step work. The fearless moral inventory is not something that folks who gravitate toward denial or blame find easy to handle.

It is important to remember that it is not what has happened to someone or what that person has done in the past that determines the outcome of his/her life. It is what a person does with the raw material of his or her life, as heinous or abusive as it might be, that determines the outcome. The only way we can use what has happened to us, and allow God to use it, is to get in touch with it.

Honesty is a challenge for many addicts and co-dependents. Lack of honesty with self and with others (step 5) is what holds people captive in their addiction and enabling. Many times this lack of honesty has allowed them to survive very difficult situations; humanly it was just too hard to face. Fear of honesty is, of course, also there because of the shame and guilt associated with the past, and it is the padlock that clinches captivity and keeps freedom at arm's length.

Manipulating others and people pleasing behaviors are survival skills for many. Beware that the desire to please you, the leader, may be part of the hamster wheel lifestyle that is still active in us all, even small group participants! As leaders, we need to pay attention to how we sit with another's pain. If we rush the process, hoping for a quick change or "right" answers, then it may be because this "sitting" is so painful. If we use our own mentors and accountability partners as safe places for us to share the pain we experience as we sit with others, we will be less likely to unconsciously fall into the trap of encouraging people to please us rather than speak honestly about their situation.

Ultimately, of course, it is the grace of God that heals us all and brings relief. In order to "get" grace we have to "get" what we have been delivered from. In order to change we must own up to old tired patterns that bring futility in the hamster wheel. Christ was all about breaking up old patterns, and his teaching was always that the truth would set us free! One of the best things leaders can do is to be authentic and honest themselves. This allows others, over time, to trust that authenticity as a way of life that is liberating.

## Session 5

For this lesson probably one of the best things you can do as a leader is to help the people in your group find someone with whom they can do an inventory who is trustworthy, safe, and who knows the Lord. Developing a sponsorship program like AA's, and training people on how to listen and be a non-judgmental presence, would be ideal.

Of course, relationships are the Velcro of all ministry and whoever is present to listen to someone's inventory must then stay in contact with the person afterward. Obviously to "drop" someone after they are honest and open is a dismissal, regardless of how non-judgmental someone is during the process. Also, the idea that this is a continual practice, not just a one-time event is a good one. So whomever someone is paired up with, they must remain a faithful friend for the long haul.

Materials for learning how to be a nonjudgmental presence can be found in Stephen's Ministry material, AA material, and in other pastoral care resources as well. Email kim@wvpc.org if you need more information on this.

It is important for you as a leader to have those to whom you can go for support who are outside of the church context in which you serve. There are days, and then there are days. No one can go it alone, and your ability to share, to vent, to confess, and to laugh with others about church snafus is paramount to your mental health. When you are working with people in recovery, there is a lot of pain and a lot of heaviness to bear. Find situations and contexts where you can share what is on your heart with laughter, tears, honesty, and openness. This will keep you fit for ministry and you will avoid the black hole of burnout. Also, always be sure that you have prayer support on an ongoing basis!

## Session 6

As in every step, sometimes you need to "fake it 'til you make it." Readers may balk at this philosophy; it sounds like lying. That can't be a God thing, can it? "Fake it 'til you make it" means something different than lying (to me). I may not be entirely willing to have God remove my defects, but I can act like I am and gradually grow into the idea that this is indeed the way to freedom. The willingness to change comes gradually and takes time. Consider the plight of parents who bring home a newborn baby – their first. The baby cries and cries and cries. These parents are weary. They perhaps wonder if they are up for the challenge. They feel like going back to bed, stuffing earplugs in their ears, and pulling the covers up over their heads. Fortunately for this defenseless baby, these fantastic parents-in-training will NOT do what they feel like, but will instead choose to do what they consider to be the next right thing. They will feed, change, and rock this little bundle whether this baby responds positively or not. In some ways, these parental units are faking it. They are doing the opposite of what their body screams for them to do.

Some days, neither facilitator nor participant wants to show up for their work. It may be helpful for a group to keep coming back to this lesson, and as we continue to practice, we will grow. Becoming self-aware involves taking a step back and reflecting. We cannot see what is wrong with a painting if we are standing so close our nose is touching it. With each backward step away, our vision of what is before us increases. But this takes time. The idea is that the more self-aware I become, the more I will realize I am functioning on the hamster wheel and need to get off. Awareness is a lifelong process, and it can all be coined under the theological term "sanctification." We never arrive. We never get there this side of heaven. We are a work in progress. So stay the course and be encouraged! The steps are a constant "work in progress".

## Session 7

In removing our shortcomings (GRACE) Jesus asks the woman to "go and sin no more." (BEING WILLING). This is the link between lessons six and seven; you may want to draw this out as you discuss this scripture.

There is definitely a paradox in this lesson (step 7) when compared to the last lesson (step 6). On the one hand, Jesus asks us to do certain things that will help us to heal and grow. On the other hand, once we begin to do those things, we realize that we can't do them on our own steam. We will fail and "miss the mark." We will add to our list of shortcomings, and we will fall again and again.

This tension is described in Galatians 2:20 when Paul says, "I, yet not I, but Christ who lives in me." So obedience to what Christ asks us to do, and at the same time, humble surrender, and asking for help daily from God and other people, go hand in hand. I mention this because as a leader, I am big on God's grace. I am always talking about the love of Jesus. People just can't get enough of this message. However, the need to "be willing" is a part of being able to receive God's grace and cooperate on a daily basis with the work of the Holy Spirit. In other words, grace and surrender don't mean passivity. They are spurs to action and cooperation with God from a heart filled with gratitude.

**Keeping the Vital Signs Up!** For us as leaders, there is a need for us to keep our spiritual vital signs up. How do we do this, when ministry can be so draining? If the church is a hospital for sinners and I am operating as a solo physician, then all will be lost. I cannot be the vital lifeline from which others get their sustenance and ability to survive. I can only lead people to the threshold...and introduce them to Jesus....supporting them as best I can. Ultimately though, they must work out their own salvation and learn ways to stay connected to God. As leaders we need to remember that this business of transformation, when it happens, has very little to do with us. It is a work of the Holy Spirit that we can point to and testify about, but as I have already emphasized, we cannot change anyone. In this line of work, we need many "time-outs."

First, we need SPIRITUAL time outs. We need at least one day every month where we can replenish ourselves and our connection to God. Maybe it is at a retreat or conference or some kind of worship experience that we are not leading.

Second, we also need FUN time outs where we can do what we love. Ministry can become duty, but as C.S. Lewis said, "Duty is the cast we put on broken love." When we stop loving our people, and we start doing because we "ought" or "should," we need to go and press the "reset" button and get our souls restored. Duty-bound ministry can become a hamster wheel. Go, go go. Do, do, do. Round and round. So...what is it that you like to do? Do it! What gets you excited, floats your boat, makes you smile, and interests you so much that for the moment it pulls you out of yourself and all the church swirl? Make it happen, and be filled with the goodness of God who created life for us to enjoy! I guarantee you will be able to love your people better if you are humble enough to admit that it is not all about what I do or don't do at the church or in ministry that makes transformation happen. It is all about God at work in weak human beings, like me, making his grace known.

**Finally…over-respond!** I will quote *No More Running In Circles…* that first step of asking for help is so difficult for survivors and critical for us to respond to. If someone reaches out to me, I assume as a rule that this may be their one and only attempt to get the help they need. The person may be drowning, and this may be their last chance to show me that they're going down. I swoop in with life rafts of supportive networks and helpful people. I sometimes overdo it, I know, and people kindly tell me that they just wanted to know when the grief and loss support group met, or how they could get a lay minister to visit a few times. I overreact because I know how difficult it can be for survivors to reach out. This may be the last time they act on the dim and fading hope that things can be different.

If someone comes to us for help, we must not ever underestimate how hard it may have been for them. We must respond with all the love we can muster.

## Session 8

As was stated before in another lesson, being real with people and honest about times when you have made amends with another is very powerful. Emphasize that making amends is an ongoing process, not something that is done just once or twice. It ought to become a rhythm for our lives – a way of doing each day – so that when I offend I immediately seek reconciliation from that person. When you share your story as a leader, this is something you may want to emphasize. If you look at creation, everything moves toward wholeness. If I skin my knee, my body moves toward mending that tear. If I cut off a branch of a tree or plant, a new one forms. Creation is postured to repair damage because it is a reflection of its Creator. When you repair a relationship, you are aligning yourself with the God who repairs, reconciles, and makes new.

I discuss in *No More Running in Circles* the fact that the difficult relationship with my mother, who was abusive, could not be amended by my going to her to try to make amends. It would have been hurtful to others, especially to my children. It is this caveat of the next step that creates difficulty sometimes – essentially that if it is harmful – don't do it. This may be something to discuss now as people reflect on where they might need to repair a relationship.

As much as I don't like to say it, and as much as I know "God is in control," my own state of mind when things don't work out the way I want (especially when it comes to ministry) is that after a time, I begin to build up a resentment against God. Now there is no way that I would ever admit this is happening and often, I don't even recognize it because the outside of me says "God works everything for good" or "God is in control." I can use these words when I am disappointed. Underneath I know that I often feel if God had wanted to help, he could have, and because he didn't I am stuck dealing with a situation that I don't want to deal with. Over the years I have flagged when this resentment begins in me. I stop praying deeply, and I stop rejoicing and expecting. After all, if God let me down that other time, what good does any of this praying and expecting do?

Phillip Yancey says that a lot of times we ask God to show up for us so that we can feel his presence, but do we really show up for God? Are we honest before him, or do we keep a pseudo spirituality going that keeps him at arm's length? I know I have been guilty of this. Over the years, I have found that wrestling with God over situations that I don't get is far better than not praying or praying superficially or simply giving up on being hopeful or expectant of the new.

This is so important for leaders in recovery, because you deal day by day with people for whom there seems to be little change and so much struggle. Sometimes you want to shout "God...DO SOMETHING!"

By wrestling I mean taking the gist of the disappointment and giving it back to the Lord by letting him see and know your disappointment, pain, anger, struggle. Be honest. Talk it out with God and other people, write it out, get mad in prayer, WRESTLE. Jacob demanded that God "bless" him; he wrestled with the angel until the morning light. Wrestle until you see that light dawn, until you truly begin to see God's plan and desire and love for people unfolding, even in part. What you don't want to do is to pull back from your relationship with God by subtly letting the passion and excitement go out of your prayer life and vision for the future. Resignation and lack of hope are signs that the enemy has worked overtime on you, probably because you were doing something right.

Simply be aware of this subtle drift toward a kind of bland resignation in your relationship with the Lord that ends up being translated into whatever ministry you are doing. Making amends to God for this drift is something I work on regularly. Wrestling helps get out my angst, and at the same time it keeps me intimate with the Almighty. Showing up for

God with all my anger and disappointment is very biblical and tracks with honesty.


## Session 9

As a leader, there are many things that we can say to our people to help them along the way. There are also great programs and opportunities that we can employ. However, over the years I have found out through hard experience what I should have known all along…that nothing transforms people more than the power of prayer. That is because in addition to dealing with the brass tacks of addiction and the complications that ensue, we are also engaged in a spiritual battle. It is a battle we cannot see, that Jesus was always referring to. We have an enemy, and the darkness of addiction is his way of stealing away people's lives.

We may know that prayer is vital, but often we do not set up our churches or programs in such a way that prayer is a priority. I am putting the emphasis on prayer in this section because as soon as you start ***doing*** love and not just talking about it (which making amends is all about) the enemy will be close at hand to discourage, distract, and create chaos.

Ask yourself the following questions to assess and begin to discover the prayer piece of doing ministry, which is the crux of all real change.

1. Do you have a prayer team, assigned to individual needs and concerns? (Sometimes one team for one person is needed if the situation is difficult.)

2. Is there a place to pray with at least two other individuals after meetings and Sunday Services?

3. Have you had prayer trainings? Do people know how to pray effectively? (God listens to all prayers, but there are ways to pray that help us focus, listen, and also discern, as well as invite the Holy Spirit in to dispel spiritual darkness.)

4. Consistency in prayer is so important. We probably won't see immediate results. Praying daily for the same thing over time yields an amazing harvest. Is there some guide or structure around consistent prayer you can provide that would be right for your people?

5. Do you have a group of people praying for you? This is so important in ministry. You need the spiritual horizon clear so that

you can move confidently forward doing love without spiritual harassment.

In sum…prayer is the conduit for change, for growth, for deliverance, and ultimately ushers in the power of the Holy Spirit. Make sure prayer happens every day, all the time, in spades!

## Session 10

If you covenant with your group to do the Prayer of Examen, this ends up being a great tool for leaders as well. As we have said earlier, getting off the hamster wheel of ministry means pausing and taking a step back. This prayer allows for reflection and review. Getting "caught up" in the work of ministry can be very valuable or very destructive. The question is always "Are we going somewhere with this program, process, or person?" Or "Are we doing the same thing over and over and expecting a different result?" In other words, the insanity of ministry is ongoing activity with no transformation and no different result. If you decide to do the Prayer of Examen, there are some important questions for leaders to ask themselves in addition to the ones mentioned in the exercise.

Did I function in this day out of a sense of joy and expectation? How might I increase my joy quotient?

Am I subtly resentful of some of the more needy people or people who have stood in my way? Ask Jesus to rid you of any resentment, even toward "church life."

What did I engage in during this day that was specifically for myself? Did I have a time-out from caring for others, and did I do something (even something as small as taking a walk) to restore my own soul?

Am I preoccupied with the future and missing the present moments – the gifts of God's presence in people – right now?

How much time have I spent praying about the things that concern me?

There may be other questions you may wish to fashion for yourself based on your particular situation. These questions have been particularly helpful to me as I have navigated the waters of ministry. I hope they are helpful to you too.

## Session 11

The exercises in today's group lesson require a leader or facilitator. Please read through ahead of time, taking note of any supplies you may need. Leaders should feel free to adapt these exercises to their own circumstances and needs based upon the make-up of the group. There is too much here for an hour and a half. Split this lesson up in the best way possible for your group's needs. If there is a favorite group prayer exercise that emerges from experimenting with these creative forms of prayer, you may want to adopt it as an opener for your gatherings on a regular basis. Give people ample time to share their experiences after each of these exercises.

One final word – as leaders, it is very difficult to convince others to practice only what we preach. But, people are often moved by our practices. And trust me, people notice what we practice.

I don't know about your situation, but I am tempted sometimes (although I cannot believe I am saying this) to think praying is slacking off. I love prayer! I love praying through God's word!

However, having four meetings in a row with folks who are in a heap of trouble feels more like my job description. Prayer takes time, and some days the tyranny of the urgent squeezes out my minutes that I have ear-marked for prayer. I've learned that when I take such an arrogant and short-sighted approach to ministry that I am rarely effective – no matter how many meetings I attend.

Let us continue to encourage each other to practice prayer.


## Session 12

One of the ways I share this new reality that we focused on in this lesson is to write material that can be used in the church to keep the stories alive and keep people moving toward growth and transformation. I would love to hear your experiences of what going through this workbook has been like for you and your people.

I am also hoping that recovery ministry can move from an adaptive model to a transformational one. By that I mean that fundamentally, if all things are possible with God, complete healing for the addict is also possible. We may all be alcoholics or co-dependents or addicts of some kind or another. However I firmly believe that ultimately there is a bigger, more glorious reality that defines us all: our identity as the beloved of God. In light of our belonging to God first, there is power in his name for the worst of us to change completely.

That is the story of Paul, and it is the story for us all. On the other hand, it is easy to wax eloquent on these issues. That is why the stories that are happening where you are ministering are where the tire hits the road, and in the end, the stories are what we all remember. So share them with me, or with people at NACR, and keep the good news of Christ's healing power alive in the hearts of God's people!

**For additional
recovery resources
visit:**

**www.nacr.org**

Made in the USA
Charleston, SC
10 March 2014